BATH BABIES

CREATING BEAUTIFUL BONDS IN WATER

JO WILSON

Contents

A drop of water
Ripples will make waves
#TogetherWeMakeADifference

To Christian, Kane, and Millie, I dedicate this book to you.

Kane and Millie, my beautiful children, you have taught me so much when we have been in the water together. I will never forget our first water memories together. So special they were, they are imprinted on my soul forever, and have given me my passion, my 'why' in life.

Christian, thank you. My husband, best friend, and soul mate.

Water rushes
Water flows
Water sprinkles on your toes
Water drips
Water splashes
Water dangles on eyelashes
Water ripples
Water runs
Water tickles on your tum
Water soothes
Water calms
Water wraps you in its arms

CHAPTER

1

INTRODUCTION

Water has always been a very special part of my life; in many ways chlorine is my choice of perfume. When I was young, I was the child who was the last to get out of the pool, wrinkled like a prune, and to this day I can recall a lot of sensory impressions and associations with water. One whiff of 'Pears Soap' and I am transported back to Sunday bathtimes.

Lots of indigenous cultures, such as those found in India, Asia, and Mexico, have customs around babies' first introduction to water, passed down from generation to generation. Massage, flower ceremonies, songs, traditional blends of oils and herbs are all commonplace. In the West, these little intricate details of knowledge and precious wisdom have been lost along the way.

As a baby swim teacher and founder of the education program *Aqua Sensory*, I know how special water can be for us all. Like a little switch, taking us from the stressed red state to the blue calm state and amplifying vibrational energies, water changes our nervous system and naturally creates mindful moments. Inside your womb, your baby became an expert in sensing the energy frequencies of muffled sound, rocking movements, and pressure. Vibration is in fact your baby's first language, so it makes sense that your baby can easily pick up on your moods, understand the tone of your voice, and interpret your touch. Although babies can't yet speak words, they can speak through their subtle body language. They sense, they feel, and they translate the language of energy vibrations, projecting their wishes and feelings back to you.

You will be exchanging beautiful sensory messages through your smell, your voice, your touch and breath.

Together we will celebrate how magical water can be. I'll guide you on how to build special water routines and rituals with your baby. My hope is that this lively interplay will provide lots of benefits for your baby's mental and physical development and deepen your bond together.

I know from supporting families at my swim school, that we can often think of bathtimes as simply *hygiene wash times,* and they can sometimes be rushed or full of overwhelm. It's my passion to unwind this notion and show you how you can make your bathtimes special.

When I was writing this book, what was very important to me from the start was ensuring you gain an understanding of bathtime from your baby's perspective, so you can create many mindful moments with them. I want to invite you to step into your baby's water world and see it through their eyes.

In this book, we will unfold how water (and bathtime) will become your best friend, helping you to bond with your baby. We will take a deep dive into why water is so special as an element for you and your baby to receive mutual delight. You might be surprised to read just why water has so many special properties and benefits for our mind and body. Your bath can become a place that allows you to heal, relax, and learn about each other, together. The bath can also be your baby's first playground.

Bath Babies is carefully researched and backed up by science and sensory know-how. Enjoy dipping and diving into this book and enjoy many splashy bathtime moments full of sensory magic and joy.

Safety mention: It goes without saying, it is always important to be with your baby when they are in or near water. Never leave your baby alone, not even for a single second. Water is a life giver and a life taker.

Side note: I often make the reference to 'your baby' in this book. I also use both genders with the pronouns he/she, as well as mothers, fathers, pregnant persons. When I refer to parents, this reference is also extended to any caregiver.

The world is changing
The way we move
The way we play
The way we connect with each other
Our lives are sometimes
thrown into the unknown
Our children feel this too
It's time to slow down
To put ourselves on pause
To iron out life's little wrinkles
And enjoy the water sprinkles.

CHAPTER

2

OUR WORLD IS CHANGING

During my many years of experience and observations as a swim teacher, I have noticed subtle changes in the way new parents handle their babies in the pool. I can also see new anxieties, society, and social media pressures. Perhaps this is because parents today feel more judged? I can feel (new) parent confidence and intuition sometimes decreasing. Do you feel this too? I often see my swim families needing more support, but sometimes finding it difficult to ask.

I know as a new mother I was often embarrassed to reach out, to ask for help. As parents and carers, we may think we 'must' struggle through with our babies, that we should 'automatically' know how to bathe them, and that nurture should always come naturally. But I know from my own personal experiences that it's easy to get intimidated by professional 'experts', side tracked by well-meaning family members full of advice based on how they parented or sucked into good old Google searches and parenting books.

Over these past years, I've also seen the greater need for community as the traditional extended family and village decreases. In response, I have started to introduce a much-needed wellbeing focus to my water programs, as the family network changes in our ever more virtual world.

My observations have led to questions, and these questions have led my curious mind to explore a way of supporting parents with their babies *before* they come to the pool. A way of nurturing and guiding my swim families so they can create special bonds with their baby, using water to support their daily routines.

It is my hope that you will find this book useful as a top up to your natural parental instincts. This book is not intended to 'teach' or 'tell' you what to do with your baby at bathtimes, it's here simply to be your friendly guide. To provide suggestions, ideas, and helpful reminders to support you, and to deepen the bond you have with *your* baby.

Babies don't come with a bathtime manual, but they do come with *you!* I look forward to introducing you to new ways to celebrate early water experiences together with your baby, and ways to create little rituals that you can celebrate together. Perhaps some will be a reminder of special water memories from your own childhood that you would like to pass onto your baby.

Our world might be changing, but the change can start with us too.

The bath is more than a
place to simply wash
It's a place for your baby to
enjoy their little swim
It's also a place to connect from within

Forget about Wi-Fi the best place
to connect is in the water

CHAPTER

3

BEAUTIFUL BONDING

It's the simple things that help you bond with your baby at bathtime. Like the way you prepare your baby's bath, the way you handle him in your loving hands, the way you talk or look at him to reassure him he is safe.

Bonding brings so many benefits to us and our babies. It's both something to cherish and seek, but don't be surprised if it takes a little time too. Bonding with our babies can help to heal our inner child, as well as support our emotional wellbeing. Research shows that bonding with your baby can help postnatal blues as the bonding process helps the brain release opioids such as dopamine, so we feel pleasure, and oxytocin, the oozy chemical of love.

The bonding process between mother and baby can start before birth, introduced before conception, and established in pregnancy. But it is equally as important to remind ourselves that a mother's bond starts with herself being kind with all the new notions of parenthood and acceptance of change. It's easy to feel fearful and to hold tension. During both pregnancy and birth, it's very easy for new mothers to forget their own needs. To nurture ourselves, to pause and attune to our developing baby is so important. But society in the West doesn't always celebrate or focus on tuning in to oneself, especially during conception, pregnancy, and birth. But the more we find this inner connection with ourselves, the more this helps the bonding process with our baby.

In our tech world, it's so easy to become disconnected, plugged in to things outside of ourselves, and not attend to the core needs that keep us grounded.

The essential notion of creating a secure attachment to a primary caregiver means in simple terms 'survival'. This is particularly important for human babies who, unlike many animals, are born prematurely in terms of their development. Within minutes of being born, most animals must be ready and able to escape danger, but human babies are unable to crawl, sit, stand, or feed themselves for several months after birth, making them more dependent on their carers than almost any other infant on the planet.

In the 1960s, the theory of attachment was brought to the forefront by Mary Ainsworth and John Bowlby. Their findings were profound and simple: healthy secure attachments with primary caregivers affects the infant's future physical and psychological development. The more securely attached we are, the more we secure our future success. Creating strong bonds with your baby doesn't just mean they will survive, but will thrive. Of course, as parents that is something that we all desire for our children.

In terms of child development theory, we used to think that *'nature'* (what we are born with) would provide us with pretty much everything we needed for healthy development, then came along the science of epigenetics. Epigenetics shows us how important environmental factors are as they will shape the way our genes express themselves. *'Nurture'* (how we are looked after) now wins the age-old debate for what is more important for optimum wellbeing and development in the critical early years window. In fact, the 1001 days of life (conception to two years) are now acknowledged as the most crucial brain sculpting years. The love and nurture our children receive in the first two years will shape their future physical and emotional development, both impacting academic success.

Let's pause and reflect on this notion: *the love and nurture we provide our babies in their first few years of life, will shape their whole future.* Wow! However, before we reflect and draw upon our own childhood experiences or be too harsh on ourselves as new parents, it's worth remembering the advice of well-known paediatrician, Donald Winnicott, that babies only require 'good enough' parenting. Your baby is ok with you not being perfect. Phew!

I love the fact that neuroscience shows us that our brain is 'plastic'. Neuroplasticity is vital for development, firing and wiring neurons together to make and strengthen connections in the brain in response to the environment and conditions around us. This means we can modify our brains and rewire adverse experiences, and it's ok to be *perfectly imperfect* as parents and caregivers. However, let's celebrate the fact that in order to thrive all your baby needs is something that is simple, something that is free: YOU, and your loving attention.

In the next chapters, I am going to guide you on how bathtimes can support you in the special bonding process. Water can be your teacher, your healer, your guide, your playmate, and classmate, in fact water is such a special element to enjoy.

Let the splashy fun times begin, as we remind ourselves that water is every baby's first home.

I am New

My birth journey matters
from conception to birth
Much more than you would ever believe
I am sensory sensitive from my new world
and all the sensations I receive.

My skin is thin and new
My cord is still healing, my
head is a bit wobbly
I love to look into your eyes
To hear your voice and be
skin-to-skin with you.

I sense your moods, vibes
are my language
I need to feel loved, seen
and heard to feel safe
I enjoy the simple things.

CHAPTER 4

FROM WOMB TO WORLD

There are so many benefits of creating strong bonds with your baby for their physical and mental health, but the best part is like water, it's free.

If we view the first few weeks of life from your baby's perspective, water can provide a perfect transition from the womb to the world. Think of water as a soft-landing cushion, from the sky dive that is your baby's birth.

The soft hydrostatic pressure of the water, together with the sides of the bath or your loving arms, feels like the safe space of the womb. It helps your baby to gain a sense of themselves, to find their centre and feel contained, soothing the aftershock of feeling separated. From the moment her cord is cut, slowly every day, step by step your baby will discover herself as an individual, separate from you.

Let's set the scene to provide a contrast from the secure, dark, warm womb to our bright, fast world. In the womb the developing foetus has *everything* they need: food, warmth, and a place to grow. At 23 weeks the foetus can swallow, find their thumb to self-soothe, can taste, can hear, and reacts to light. The developing foetus is being soothed by their mother's heartbeat, muffled voice, and gentle movements. These constant sensory signals feed into the brain, firing the neurons to make new connections. With a constant temperature and in darkness, the amniotic waters of the womb provide sensory harmony.

The transition from the womb to the world can be quite a startling experience for most babies. They must get used to their new bright world and work hard not to feel overstimulated by all the new sensations. Human babies' physical bodies are still very immature. Their digestive, immune, circulatory, respiratory, and nervous systems are not ready for our world. It therefore takes up a lot of their energy to regulate in this new world, and to cope with all its new demands. For some babies it can be a sudden shock to their immature systems, which are activated all at once. But this is where you can really help, by being sensitive to your baby's new experiences and holding them dearly in your care. The water can also be there as your friendly guide.

The first few weeks after birth are often termed the 'fourth trimester', and it's a period of big adjustment for you and your baby. Try to enjoy wallowing in the first few weeks of your baby's birth. Find time to hold space for yourself, as well as your baby.

Often as new parents we do not fully celebrate that we have brought a new magical soul into the world. There is something so refreshing and powerful about embracing and not rushing the special fourth trimester. It's time to heal together. Gently remind yourself that your baby is learning so much by regulating themselves into their new world, through you.

It will be your instinct to protect your baby. At times you may feel worried, you may question if your baby is enjoying their bath. Of course, we all want what's best for our baby. Know you are not alone in these feelings. It is my hope that with the information in this book you can feel more certain and will be able to find your own rhythm with your baby. Celebrate your baby's uniqueness, and yours too.

Know you are doing such a great job, because you are doing your best. Know that the bath can become your special place to feel calm and grounded. Whatever emotions arise from you and your baby, meet them just where they are.

Your special sensory water journey starts here.

Free yourself from the flutter and clutter
Soften and heal from the inside out
Find your inner flow
Enjoy watching your baby grow

CHAPTER

5

MINDFUL MOMENTS

Mindfulness has become popular in recent years, perhaps because it's the perfect antidote to our new fast-paced, and often stressed world.

Mindfulness is a state of being fully present in the body, a time where we can switch off the daily noise from thoughts and remain at peace with ourselves. We are present, more aware, and able to view the world around us from a more compassionate lens. It's also a practice, as often our mind will pull us away and back into busy, racing thoughts again. Know that this is ok! Quite normal in fact, even monks who are masters at meditation observe passing thoughts. The first stage of mindfulness is being aware of our thoughts, and then being able to switch back into creating space in our mind. Often the breath is used as the anchor to create mindfulness. We can focus on the in-breath and extend our out-breath to provide a sense of inner calm.

Mindfulness is not often associated with baby bath-time. In this chapter, we explore a little mindful practice we call our 'check in'. Being more mindful in our actions and thoughts strengthens our sense of self awareness, which we can pass on to our baby.

Everything starts with a sense of ourselves. We are all unique human beings, souls ready to experience life. When life can feel challenging, our sensory systems can be out of sync. In her book *Balanced and Barefoot*, Angela Hanscom explains how our modern world is experiencing a rise in sensory processing disorders and decline in play, which in return is having an impact on mental health.

Let's start our water times with a little check in and a mindful relaxation practice.

It's important we start with ourselves. You might not be aware just how much your baby feeds off your emotional state. Our feelings are often stored in our posture, breath, and our body language. Whether you are feeling relaxed or a little tense, your baby will sense this.

Know that you are also your baby's safe harbour; your actions are a mirror. This mirror will provide meaning to your baby, so they are able to make sense of their new world. Before your baby can explore their world, they will need to feel safe and to trust their environment. In other words, you act as a 'bridge' between your baby and their experiences in the world. You could even think of yourself as their personal shock absorber.

Before you start your baby's bathtime, observe and tune into your own feelings and needs.

Enjoy this little check in practice

Spend a moment finding your centre. Take a breath in, tune into the ambient sounds, lightly close your eyes for just a moment (ensuring your baby is in a safe place for you to do so), and maybe place your hand on your heart if that feels good for you. This has a natural way of regulating and slowing down our heart rate and breathing. This little check in practice may only take a moment, but it is so powerful! It helps us to slow our actions down, switching us from an auto-pilot mode, or a mode where we are feeling rushed, to one that is more mindful and conscious.

You can do this check in as you get your baby's bath ready.

When I play with water
I learn to listen
I learn to move my body in new ways
I learn to communicate what I enjoy
To feel the water
To let go and float
When I play with water
I learn how to love water

CHAPTER

6

WONDERFUL WATER

Bonding with your baby happens naturally every time you are with your baby providing for their needs, but when we add in water, that's when the magic can happen.

Together let's explore why water is so wonderful, and why bathtimes are the perfect place to deepen bonds.

Water has many magical benefits for humans that are unique compared to when we are on land. When we are in water we float, we can move effortlessly and freely in many more ways than we can on land, and we feel calmer as the water exerts a gentle pressure on our bodies, like a little water hug.

Water and the human vibrational energy are the perfect partners, as water provides a faster energy transfer. Babies are primed to pick up on our mental and emotional states, and when in water our vibrational field *'magnifies'*. You may find that when in or near water, your baby is more sensitive to your moods and emotions, or you are to theirs.

Are you familiar with the 'Blue Mind' theory? The Blue Mind theory, created by marine biologist Wallace Nichols, is the theory that being in or near water can alter the state of our nervous systems, from the stressed state to a state of calm, which releases feel-good hormones. And of course that, coupled with the fact that when we are in the bath there are far fewer modern distractions, makes it easier to become more mindful.

Water is naturally multi-sensory, and playful stimulation for you and your baby. There are many tastes, smells, sounds, and tactile delights to discover and explore. Spend a moment tuning into the simple way light bounces and reflects off water or listen to simple water sprinkles or splashes. Water is very playful. Splash water and it will splash you right back. Dry land is so boring in comparison! It doesn't respond like water. Often babies are mesmerised by the properties of water. Do you find this with your baby too? Are they curious when in or near water?

Water amplifies the senses

We *feel* more when we are in water. Water triggers our nervous systems, amplifying our senses. Our bodies and minds process the multitude of sensory sensations, all at the same time. Water has a very special way of (naturally) creating a beautiful body and mind connection.

Did you know, we are in fact water! Well at least 70% or so, and even more so for your baby. Without water there is no life. I truly believe we need to protect water, our beautiful blue planet. When we love water, we are not only protecting our planet for our children who are the next generation, but we are also loving ourselves.

It's my vision and my gift to you, to pass on my experiences, so you too love water and pass this onto your baby. Our blue planet needs us right now.

Let's take a moment to thank water for giving and providing us with life.

Water is of course a life giver and a life taker. It goes without saying we must always supervise our babies as even just a few inches of water can be dangerous and a source of drowning.

Water feels like home

Bringing your baby back to the water can be like bringing them home, having spent the last nine months in the warm amniotic waters of the womb. Water holds memories. Your baby will be able to feel and remember so much more than you think when they are immersed in water. Water has a way of unlocking subtle generational whispers that were once forgotten. Water immersion for newborns can therefore be like their little therapy.

In later chapters, I'll show you how to allow and guide your baby to unfold, to integrate, to heal and transition into our bright, bold world through the magic of water.

How does water make you feel?

Can you remember your first water experiences? Were they fun-filled or full of fear?

When we give ourselves the time and space to notice how we are feeling when we are in water, we can honour and nurture ourselves, and even heal. To be able to check and tune into what we are feeling is of course a practice all by itself. We might feel joy, fear, or frustration. Break any cycle of comparison to other parents and do ask for support if you feel anxious when bathing your baby. When we are in any fear-based cycle, we are unable to fully embrace the experience; it is easy to become overwhelmed and your baby will feel this through you too.

Water has a clever way, through its energy and vibrations, of reflecting how we are feeling. Being able to understand ourselves, accept our mistakes, and embrace challenges is one of the beautiful gifts that water can provide.

Let's reflect

How does water make you feel?

Does it make you feel calm or playful? Does it help free your mind and body? We all have a personal relationship to water. It can hold our emotions and even memories. Take time to explore and find ways to be in water that feel good to you.

The transition to parenthood isn't always smooth. Water times could become your time to socialise with your baby *and* create a mindful moment to simply be.

A little space to write what comes up for you

The sounds of happy babies
Playing, happy, splashing
Soak them up
Store them
In your happy memory bank
Retrieve them when you need them
Your heart will surely soar!

CHAPTER

7

MY FIRST BATH

Together, let's make your first water experiences special for you and your baby. It's so easy to rush through bathtimes quickly, with little or no conscious thought. Just another task on the daily list to tick off, something that we simply do. Let's take a step back, I promise the outcome you feel will be so different. Without the rush, together in your arms, your baby will feel safe, calm, and content.

Your first baths can be the perfect place to heal from birth. In your loving arms, and hearing your soothing voice, it's the perfect transition for your baby from womb to world.

Most babies will enjoy a simple top and tail wash in their first week as their umbilical cord heals and their sensitive skin transitions from the womb to the outside world. So, allow yourself to be guided by your intuition as to when it's the right time to bath your baby.

Giving your baby their first bath may be met with a little anticipation. How are you feeling? Nervous or excited? How do you think your baby is feeling? Baby's first bath doesn't have to be very long, but it does need to be mindful and slow. Think quality over quantity.

The best time to bathe or play with your baby is when they are in a *calm-alert* state. You will recognise this state as their body will be relaxed, their breathing regular. They will enjoy looking at your face and listening to your voice. They are attentive, their eyes are bright, and they will be ready for their bath. It is good to recognise when your baby is ready, rather than forcing bath and water times at a set point in the day.

Some babies prefer morning baths, others like one before bedtime, and lots of babies enjoy baths in the daytime too, when they are rested and ready for a little playtime.

When your baby is in their calm-alert state they will be able to process sensory information better, organise themselves, learn new things, and make sense of their world.

Does your baby enjoy swaddles and close cuddles? They will probably enjoy the feeling of being wrapped in a big cloth or muslin, to feel contained like in their first water home, the womb.

Water time is about more than just getting clean. Yes, babies all need a bath at times, just like they will need their nappy changed. But this is a time for connection, not distress. If you see your baby pulling away or crying, wait a moment. Calm your baby, decide if this is the right time and if you can wait, or simply provide a little cloth wash instead.

I can feel it too
The love between us
The connection and the calm
When you are snuggled in my arms

The water is waiting to receive us
Let's allow water to be our teacher
Together we are both
learning all the time

CHAPTER

8

THE 5 C'S

An easy way to remember how to create beautiful bath-time experiences is to follow the 5 C's:

> Consent - permission, is your baby saying yes?
> Containment - baby will love to feel contained
> Calming - slow and mindful movements
> Connection - we all need to belong
> Check in - how are you and your baby at this moment?

CONSENT

Being truly baby-led means your baby has autonomy over their body. We always check that they are ready for their bath by tuning into their body language, gestures, sounds, and responses. Being mindful and paying attention to these cues helps us understand and respond to how they are feeling.

CONTAINMENT

In the womb, your baby received unconditional love from the safe containment of the womb space, their first home. Containment shapes our emotional process of understanding and feeling safe. During your baby's bath, you will find many of our holds and moves provide the feeling of containment. They can help prevent your baby becoming overwhelmed.

CALMING

The optimum state for your baby is for them to feel nice and calm. Bath Babies considers all the transitions in *and* out of the bath, and provides slow and mindful holds and moves to keep your baby feeling calm.

CONNECTION

"Connection has the power to counterbalance adversity." - Bruce Parry.

As humans, we need connection to feel whole. Building special relationships with each other, and using our senses to explore the environment around us, helps us to create this sense of connection that is so vital for our wellbeing. Babies start building connections with the world and those around them right from day one, soaking everything up and storing it within, and bathtime is an opportunity to deepen their connection with you and water.

CHECK IN

Is this the right time for a bath? Check if your baby is healthy and happy to receive their bath. If they are unwell, it is best not to bathe your baby.

Be comfortable in yourself, your clothes, and where you are setting up your bath. Are you on the floor or at a table so it is at your height, or in the big bath? Be aware of your mood and how much time you have.

Wash your hands and take off any sharp rings or other jewellery.

Your baby will be working overtime to process all the sensory stimuli in their environment. Whilst we as adults can easily filter out distractions, your baby's brain is learning how to habituate and filter out the information they do not need. It's a good idea to talk softly and to keep noise levels low. Loud sounds can be startling for your baby and distracting.

Choosing the right bath

Choosing the right bath to buy for your baby is a personal preference; if you even need a baby bath at all. The big bath (shared with you) provides the perfect bathing experience, which we talk about in our co-bathing chapter.

One thing is for sure, babies grow quickly, so bear this in mind when deciding what to use for bathtime. Investing in a simple plastic tub is fine, with a towel at the base for extra comfort.

Swaddles

A large muslin cloth can be a great way to wrap your baby, keeping them snuggly and contained whilst in the bath. Tuck one of their arms in and leave the other for them to self-soothe if they wish.

Our little pointers below will help you to prepare the environment from your baby's perspective and to provide a sense of calm:

- Turn down the lights so there are no bright overhead lights
- Clear away any shampoos, tubs, and clutter around the bathing area
- Turn off any background noise from the TV/ radio, and make sure your phone is on silent
- Ensure the room has a neutral smell or burn a candle with a gentle scent like lavender, to enhance the feeling of calm
- Have two towels at the ready for your baby
- Check the water temperature is body temperature and the ambient air temperature feels warm
- Newborn babies' skin is very sensitive, so just use water at first in their bath

- Don't forget, you are the other important ingredient. Did you take your mindful moment to check into your breath? How do you feel? Is this the best time for you both to enjoy bathtime?
- Wear comfortable clothing you can move in

Less is often so much more for your baby, enjoy this perfect time to connect and bond.

Hey little one
You are safe in my arms
As you look up to the stars
Know you are safe
Know you belong
Know I am here for you
Know you are celebrated
Just as you are
And for all you are meant to be

CHAPTER

9

BATHTIME HOLDS AND MOVES

How to hold and handle your baby in the bath may come naturally to some parents, but for others it can take a little bit of experimenting to find what works. As long as your baby's needs are being met, it doesn't matter whether it comes instantly or requires a bit of practice. Remember that bathtime is a new activity for your baby *and* it's also a new experience for you as a new parent.

When you are handling and supporting your baby in their bath, you are sending love through your hands. As you handle your baby tune into your hands, visualise yourself relaxing, allow your hands to feel the support your baby needs. We call this 'their just right support'. Visualise your baby relaxing through your hands as you say your soft words of love.

Use your breath if you wish, so you feel in sync and in flow with your baby as you move them in their bath.

I hope you enjoy the holds and moves from our program, Bath Babies. Here are some of our parents and babies' favourites.

- **Let's start with a safe little entry into the bath.**

Upright Cradle

As you lower your baby into the bath, a nice position for them to be in is an upright cradle hold. Your whole arm should be supporting your baby as they rest their head snug into your elbow, or if you prefer, position one hand on their head and one hand on their bottom. Support your baby gently with soft, relaxed hands, and lower them into the water, bottom first.

Babies' genitals are super sensitive, so go slowly. Observe any little startles as you lower them into the water further. This upright cradle hold is ideal for safe entry into the water, and for your baby to feel naturally contained and secure. You can also vary this hold and position by having your baby more upright or lying down a little.

Finding My Feet

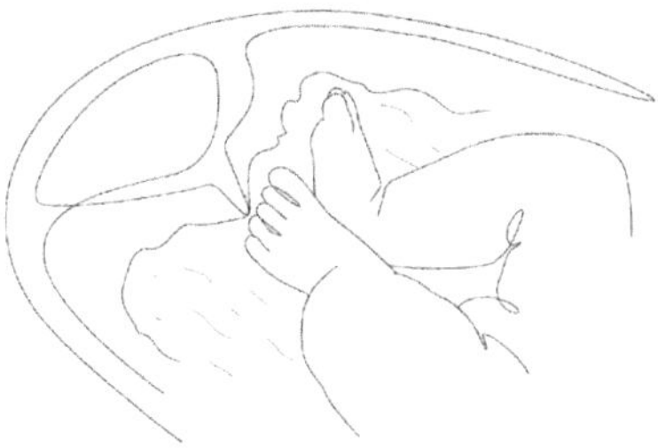

Babies are born with thousands of tiny nerve receptors in their feet (7,000 in fact), which means they are super sensitive to touch and tickles, so they often prefer a firm touch on their feet.

Position your baby's feet flat against the end of the bath, with a little pressure. Because babies don't yet fully understand that they have feet, legs etc, having their feet touching the end of the bath helps activate their proprioceptive sense, sending signals to the brain to say where their body is orientated.

Their brain asks....

- Am I sitting down or sitting up?
- Where does my body end?

The simple act of having their feet touching the end of the bath helps begin to answer these questions.

The gentle pressure on the soles of the feet also stimulates all the nerve endings and reflex points in the foot, and increases the energy flow through their body. This allows your baby to relax more, to feel contained and safe. You may start to see them enjoying pushing off the side of the bath.

This little hold and move has the added benefit of being what's called a 'brain mapping move' as one side of the body talks and connects to the other, firing little sensory signals via a feedback loop. The more your baby moves, the more their brain and body learns as it is through movement that our babies build an internal map of how to orient themselves. One little motor skill builds on another, rolling, sitting, walking etc.

Simple Sprinkles

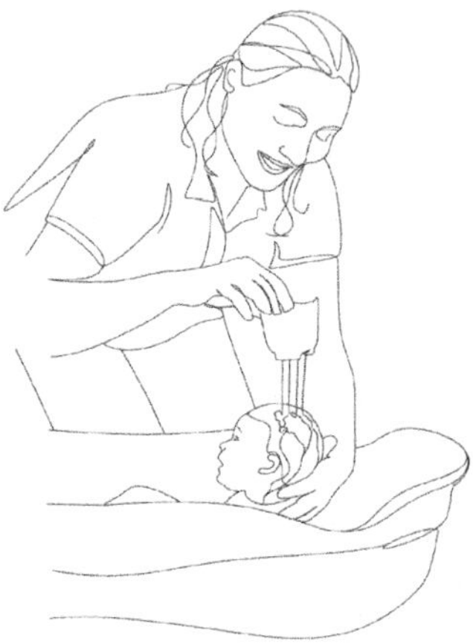

Be mindful of the soft part of your baby's head, their fontanelle. Gently cup the back of their head with your open palms. Use a cup or small jug to pour little simple water sprinkles, from the *back* of their head, using just a very small amount of water at first. Watch the water lightly fall down their face, like a little water kiss and *not* a waterfall!

The intention of simple sprinkles does not always have to be one of hygiene and washing. You can also use simple sprinkles across their body too, from their head to their shoulders, to their knees, and to their toes. Talk to your baby as you sprinkle. Name the body parts in a sing-song voice as your baby will be learning all about themselves as you sing.

Care and consideration is needed when pouring water around your baby's face. When washing their hair, start to pour the water from the *back* of their head. Gently caress and stroke your baby's hair as you wash them. They will receive your love at the same time as their little hair wash.

Often it can feel strange talking out loud to our babies, but the more you try it (almost like a running sports commentary on what's happening), the more natural it feels.

Why is this important for your baby, you may ask? Your baby needs to know what's happening to them to feel safe. Let's think about bathtime from their perspective. Their world feels new, and at the same time most of their movements are reflexive; they are still working out how their body fully works. Your baby relies totally on you to make sense of their world. Talking to them about what's happening might seem a small thing to us, but it's of enormous benefit to your baby.

Heart Talk

Your baby has an inbuilt system that syncs their emotions to yours through your body language, gestures, posture, the way you smile and handle your baby. These little transmissions and the energy within you will be giving your baby unspoken messages. You can provide little positive messages of love through your hands and your heart. In Bath Babies, we call this Heart Talk.

Try this: Simply rest your hand on your baby's chest and say your Heart Talk words out loud, in a whisper, or even just as a simple thought. Make sure your baby is looking at you as you say your words of love.

Here are a few of our favourite Heart Talk messages:

> *You are safe*
> *I see you*
> *I hear you*
> *I love you*
> *We are connected*

Baby Float

Place one hand gently on your baby's bottom and the other softly, but with a flat open palm, under their head. Gently lower your baby into the water, submerging their ears. Explain to your baby what you are doing and observe their response.

> *"We are going for a little float, is that nice?"*
> *"How does that feel?"*

Often parents worry about their baby's ears getting wet and being under the water, but it is quite safe, unless your health professional has advised otherwise due to any ear conditions.

The Baby Float position provides your baby with the perfect back, neck, and spine alignment. Most babies will enjoy their float, they will feel calm and deeply relaxed.

Observe your baby, again tuning into her signals. This will show your baby you are attuning to her needs, and that you understand her.

Observe her hands and feet, do they look relaxed, or tense and open? Is your baby engaged with you, or gazing away? Taking a little break?

You can vary the water depth for the Baby Float position. Try a shallow bath at first, then a deep one and see which one your baby prefers.

The more you fill the bath with water, the more this will allow your baby to free float, whilst a shallow water bath, with a towel at the bottom for comfort, will allow your baby to rest on the bottom of the bath. Allow your baby to wiggle, to twist and turn. The water can provide a connection back to their first home, their birth, and an embodied somatic experience for them to unfold.

Swoosh

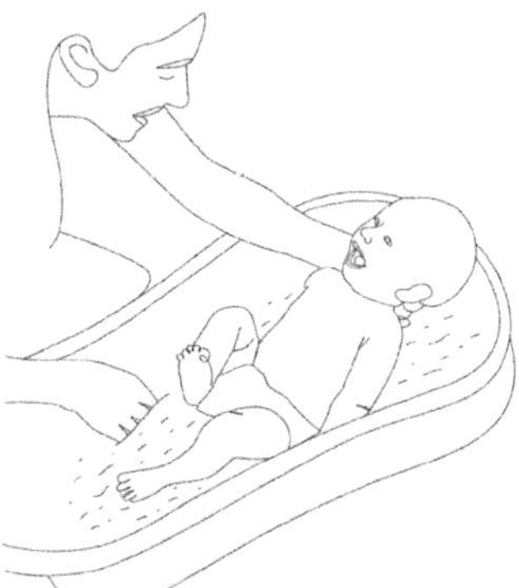

All babies seem to like this hold and move, regardless of their age and developmental stage. I hope yours does too.

Sit or float your baby in the bath and move them backwards and forwards. The swoosh gently stimulates the vestibular system, which is important for their balance and their posture.

The back-and-forth movement, coupled with the water making little waves, will provide your baby with an extra layer of stimulation and a little water massage too.

Start with a slow swoosh, then try a fast one. Observe your baby closely, he will show you his preference.

Tune into his facial expression, gaze, and sounds. Which bathtime move did they prefer, a fast or a slow swoosh?

You can also add in a sensory layer with your breath, that can feel nice for you too. Take a little breath in and say and extend the word, s-w-o-o-s-h, as you breathe out. A relaxing moment for both of you. A little ah-ha moment.

Close Connections

You may soon come to realise your newborn baby is fascinated by your face and your voice. In the bath, hold him so your face is close to his, at about 20-30cm distance. A newborn baby's sense of hearing is well-developed at birth but their world is fuzzy, as their sight is still developing, so it is good to hold them close.

He hears sounds and can pick up on their tone, pitch, and rhythms. He will be comforted by lullabies and will enjoy your singsong 'parentese' voice.

Your sing-song parentese voice will set the tempo, and a slow tempo will make him feel calm. It's a good idea to say the same bathtime words and songs each time as you will find your baby enjoys the predictability and it will help them feel reassured.

It might seem funny at first, talking to your baby and letting her know what you are doing, but not to your baby. Imagine someone doing something new to you, you may tense, waiting and anticipating what is going to happen next. It is the same for your baby. They love your voice, and will emotionally feel into its reassuring sound and tone

These close connections and moments of mutual gaze are important shared bonding moments. As you and your baby stare into each other's eyes, science and research shows us that this is an important process for communication, as your brain waves fall in sync.

Bathtimes are so much fun!

Cuddle and close

When your baby is saying it's time to get out now, have two towels at the ready. Place one over your shoulder and the other around your baby as you gently lift them out of the bath.

Avoid any sudden movements, like placing them on the floor or a changing table.

A rule of thumb is the smaller they are, the slower you move. This is a B-I-G transition for your baby, from the warm water back to the dry world again.

Your baby will enjoy being close to you, keep him snuggled in a towel and gently pat him dry. We call this hold and move our Cuddle and Close, it provides your baby with a nice end to her bath time.

Feel into her needs, she may be showing you she is tired or needs a little feed.

Time to Play

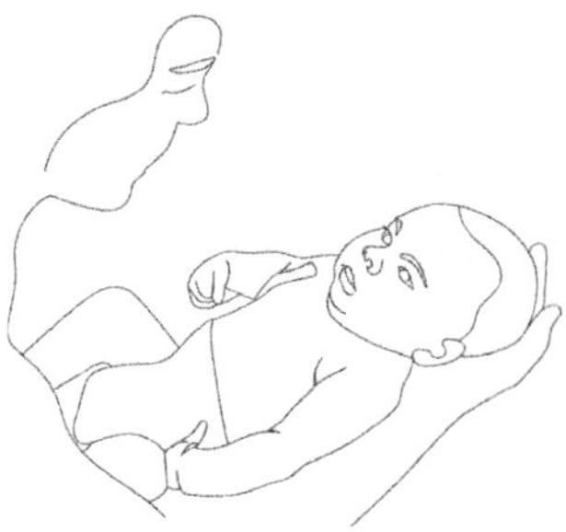

Does your bathtime have time to pause for play? To splash and play with the water or to kick a ball? I invite you to observe what your baby likes and dislikes. To provide them the space to freely move and to provide them with a range of bathtime activities. Playing in the bath doesn't have to be complicated, full of toys, or noisy. Bathtime can be just the water, with a few little play prompts.

Let's explore a few together.

Play prompts:

- Easy eye contact
- Soft hands
- Mindful moves
- Sing song voice
- Make little water waves
- Words to prompt actions: splash hands, kick feet
- Add in a little ball for bath time fun
- Cuddles and after bath snuggles

Keep in mind bathtimes are like all activities, some holds and moves your baby will enjoy more than others, and that's okay. Each bathtime will be different, just as all babies are different. As your baby grows, so too will their bathtime experience.

A little space to write about you and your baby's favourite bath time holds and moves

As your body meets mine
I love to feel your warmth
I love to see your smile
I love to hear your voice
In the bath we are in flow
Sensory harmony in action

CHAPTER

10

BATHING TOGETHER

Lots of my swim parents love co-bathing together, but some haven't even thought to try it. Bathing together can bring you the ultimate bonding experience. Think of it as an extension of 'Kangaroo care'.

There is overwhelming evidence that Kangaroo care improves infant mental health and sleep patterns, as well as supporting weight gain, which is why it is recommended for preemie babies - many of whom have been reported to have been able to leave hospital sooner than expected. One Canadian study also reported that preemie babies who received Kangaroo care also received more brain stimulation.

When your baby is next to you skin-to-skin they can regulate their heart with yours, they feel safe next to your body. Being immersed in water with you brings your baby closer to their first home. You were their safe container that provided them with everything they needed.

If you haven't tried co-bathing, perhaps it's because you feel you need another pair of hands. While this can help, it is not totally necessary, but *always be guided by how safe and confident you feel.* Gently lower yourself into the bath first, then kneel and lean over to gently pick up your baby. I recommend you have your baby in a bouncy chair to make it easier. The water temperature needs to be body temperature (36-37 degrees Celsius), which may feel a little cool to you, but perfect for babies as it's important their bath is not too hot.

Rest your baby on their back, against your chest. A little note of caution: watch where the water line is and make sure it's not lapping in their ears.

Breathe together.

Enjoy this moment to rest and relax.

If your baby would like to see you or sit up, turn them around so they are on your front where they can see you, or sit them up facing you.

You can also use a small cup to create little water sprinkles. Your baby will enjoy feeling the water flow around their body.

Here is one of my favourite rhymes to show your baby how you love the water, with the added benefit of building body awareness too.

> *"Sprinkle your fingers, sprinkle your toes,*
> *sprinkle your tummy and sprinkle my nose."*

Have you ever tried feeding your baby in the bath? If they are a little hungry you don't have to get out of the bath, feed in the water - ensuring the water line is not near their mouth. This has the added benefit of feeding their physical and emotional needs at the same time. Bottle and/or breast, the choice is yours. But, I know many breastfeeding mums found this practice reassuring as their milk flowed more. Being skin-to-skin promotes the milk-making hormones.

In the bath together, your baby will 100% feel your presence and it can be a place for both of you to fall deeper in love. It's the ultimate space where they can be totally with you, receiving 100% of your nurturing touch.

Bathtime is also the simplest but most amazing sensory experience for them. They will be able to gaze into your eyes, hear your soothing words, tune into your heartbeat, they will naturally be exchanging your smell. All of which promotes the production of the love and bonding hormone, oxytocin. This is sensory harmony in action.

If you are having a challenging day, co-bathing can be a wonderful reset. The perfect antidote to our modern day life, full of hustle and bustle, as our bodies will take over and be the loving supporting container for our babies. We will come back home, back into balance, connect with ourselves, our baby, and the water.

The biggest change is for mothers. Have you paused and thought how marvellous your body was to carry and create human life? What is not often talked about is our body image, how we view ourselves. Our body and mind are so intertwined. One of the positives of co-bathing is we can tune into our inner selves and marvel at just how our bodies change and transition.

But there is of course change for all family members and bathtimes can also be family together times.

Beautiful Body Love Practice

Let's not overlook our bodies, but celebrate them.

With your baby resting on you, mind map your body parts from your toes, legs, tummy, chest, arms, and head, giving thanks to each body part. Bringing the mind into focus and relaxing that body part at the same time.

On a physical and psychological level this practice has many benefits.

Feel into this beautiful body love practice and feel any stresses melt away, as you reduce any build-up of the stress hormone, cortisone.

Tune into your breathing patterns, slowing down.

On an emotional level, your brain's neurotransmitters will be releasing endorphins, dopamine, serotonin, and flooding you with the love hormone, oxytocin. It's important we love ourselves, but how often do we stop and do this?

Self-love will give you greater confidence and ripple out to your baby too. But what is so magical about practising beautiful body love in water compared to dry land, is that water amplifies the energy vibrational field. As mentioned before, vibrations are your baby's first language, and babies are particularly sensitive to them. Although this can be practised anywhere, in water you will be giving you and your baby greater benefits.

A little mantra for you and your beautiful body

A mantra is a sound vibration that travels through your body, it is a mindful practice that connects mind, body and soul. You don't have to be spiritual to feel the power of mantras.

One of my favourites is …

> *I am loving awareness ... (Ram Dass)*
> *I'm perfect the way I am....*

Breaking the cycle

As parents we are sometimes our own worst critics. It's easy to build fears from past experiences, to have self-doubt. We can hold onto emotions, like water in a little bucket. In the bath, we can use the water as an anchor to release and let go. We can do this by giving ourselves the time and the space to explore with compassion our worries and feelings, which in return will allow us to know ourselves better. This helps break the cycle of transferring any anxieties onto our baby, which can be a whole little practice all in itself.

Whilst in the warm water, set your intention of what you would like to release.

What is no longer serving you? Take a breath in for 4 counts, feel your tummy rise and watch the water swirl. Slowly breathe out for 8. Let go of any sensations, like tension and any emotions that you would like to release. Feelings like frustration and anxiety can soften in the water. Allow them to be washed away.

Know you are everything your baby needs.

Your baby is a multidimensional little one
He feels in more ways than one
She understands in more ways than one
He moves, plays, and loves
in more ways than one

While water gently unfolds
more of who they are

We wait
We watch
We wonder

While supporting them
They become themselves

CHAPTER

11

BABY-LED BATHTIMES

What do we mean by being 'baby-led'? Surely we must lead as parents, after all we know what's best for our baby and when they need to have a bath!? How can our baby let us know how they are feeling and what they need when they can't talk? These are a few common questions I often get asked as an educator.

Baby Signals

Don't underestimate your baby's understanding, they are conscious little souls and although they may not have their own words, they do have their own language.

Your baby will have their own way of telling you how they feel in the water. They'll let you know when they are content and when they would like more, when they are getting a little tired and when they have had enough. These little behaviour signals are what we call 'cues'. Through gentle observation, and through your loving bathtimes, getting to know your baby will increase her comfort and joy.

Some of your baby's cues will be more subtle than others. Let's unpack a few together from your baby's perspective.

> **I am having fun**: I will lean forward, curious to explore, my body is soft and relaxed. My movements are smooth, I love to focus on your eyes and voice. Sometimes, it's so much fun so I let you know my contentment through my little gurgles and giggles.
>
> **I am getting tired now:** oooh hold me, I need more water hugs right now. Do you notice my little frown or me looking away? I'm breaking your gaze so I can regulate the stimulation in my world right now. To help me soothe I love sucking my fingers. When my systems inside feel funny I often hiccup, yawn, or cough. I'm working overtime to regulate my autonomic sensory systems. When I feel very fussy, it is time to slow down. I'm ready to finish my water session with you.
>
> **I am ready to stop:** you might notice my skin colour starts to change. Sometimes I react by going pale, other times my skin goes blotchy or red. This is a sign that my sensory systems are a little stressed and overloaded right now. Notice also my breathing changing as my body tenses. Notice my hands and feet clench, I'm showing

> you signs I'm overwhelmed. Help and support me when I cry. Tune in, it might be time for my feed, sleep - it's time to respond to my needs.

Sensory Thresholds

Notice your baby's needs, and how they interpret sensory information. Babies don't come with a bathtime manual. Every baby is unique. What works for one baby, may be very different to another. Little babies are sensitive and can easily be overwhelmed. Think of every sensory stimulus as a layer: movement, water, your voice, bright lights, scents. Less is definitely more in the first few weeks for your baby. And it is worth noting that premature babies are more sensitive and can become over-stimulated more easily than full-term babies.

Enjoy getting to know your baby and learning how to support them. Vary the sensory layers and levels of stimulation in his new water world.

Momma, thank you for seeing me
Letting me know it's ok
I have faith in you

Nothing feels better than to be with you
I am grateful that you sense my moods
I love our water times together
Relaxing together
I appreciate all that you do!

CHAPTER

12

WHAT HAPPENS IF ....?

Nothing is perfect, in fact allow bathtimes with your baby to be imperfectly perfect, babies don't come with a manual, but they do come with *you.*

> *When experiences are new, like bathtimes, it is ok to feel a little nervous, for both of you. Surrender your expectations.*

Your baby will build up their preferences, enjoy tuning into these. But also, be aware, it's easy for us all to load experiences with emotions. "He doesn't like his bath." "She enjoyed it so much more last time, I must have done something wrong." Try to meet all bathtimes neutrally, with no pre-set judgements.

Let's explore a few of the most common parent questions that you might have.

Pooping: For some babies the water will be providing the internal digestive systems with a little massage, so it will be natural for your baby to have a poo. Most parents find that their baby doesn't poo in the bath, however if your baby does, gently lift them out and snuggle with a towel, whilst you use clean water as a hygiene wash.

Slippy: In water, a baby's skin can feel nice and smooth, even a little slippy. Unless your baby needs a special oil or lotion, do not put anything on your baby's skin during their bathtime. Position your hands gently but securely. Ask yourself, what feels good for you and what feels good for your baby? It is ok to try different positions. Your baby will forgive you if at first their water time feels a little clumsy. Allow repetition and growing experience to be your guide.

Cries and doesn't like it: In most cases, it is my shared experience that the majority of babies do enjoy their bath and water times. If there are unhappy sessions, don't let this set you back. There will be many new opportunities to try again. Mistakes may happen, splashes or slips, but that is ok, your baby will understand that you are both learning together.

Release and let go

If you find your baby is building up a cycle of crying during their bathtimes, start to tune in and wonder why. Try new times of the day, observe their state: are they just too tired or hungry? Would they prefer a big bath or shower with you? The biggest reassurance you can provide your baby is you.

Set an intention

When we set an intention we are connecting with purpose to a chosen emotion or desired way of being. It's like a guiding principle for how you want to show up in the world. A bathtime intention could be to create a lovely bath that is short and sweet, or to give your baby a nice calm feeling before bedtime to soothe them and help them sleep. Each bathtime will be different, tune into your baby's feelings and set your intention accordingly. Surrender yourself to the moment and what will simply be and try to meet your baby where they are developmentally, physically, and emotionally.

Create your intention at the start of bathtimes, from your heart. When you are bathing your baby, they will naturally feel close to you. They will be able to feel your love and you will be able to tune into their needs, relieve their stress and return their smiles.

> *I intend to trust you, like you trust me*
> *I intend to be in this moment*
> *I intend to bath you with my love*

In water, your relationship together is mutually beneficial, like a little colourful coral and amazing algae in perfect symbiosis.

I love my bathtime routine
I love the familiar
I love repetition
It's not boring for me
It's how I learn
It's how I feel safe
It will allow me to feel calm
From the inside out

CHAPTER

13

WATER ROUTINES AND RITUALS

Water ceremonies across the world dating back thousands of years were used to hold sacred blessings and spaces. Try it and feel the power yourself.

The Indigenous Nahuatl water ritual is a ceremony where individuals honour water as a life-giving, spiritual force by presenting offerings, singing, and performing dances in the water.

Humans and animals are naturally drawn to water and build their home around water as their central grounding community foundation. Water is deeply respected, celebrated and blessed in many cultures, something not truly appreciated in the West, where water is treated as a commodity and not valued. I hope this will change in the future, and my hope is that this book may provide you with a new or deeper awareness and appreciation of water, that you can pass onto your baby.

Let's celebrate water together and learn from other cultures who value water.

We can do this by creating little routines and rituals.

The words 'routine' and 'ritual' are often placed together, but let's unpack the benefits of both for you and your baby when bathing.

Routines

Routines create predictable patterns of behaviour for your baby, which is important because the brain needs predictability, exposure, and repetition to feel safe.

Predictability allows us to trust our environment. Exposure allows the brain to make new brain synaptic pathways - these little signals can actually be seen in brain scans as tiny sparks - and repetition is needed to produce strong brain connections. So, when you take the time to create a loving routine around bathtime your baby will not only have a fun and bonding experience, but they will also develop a sense of security and enjoy all these beautiful brain benefits.

Create your own routine but try where possible to create your intentions in both a meaningful way and in the same order.

Prepare your bathroom, dim lights, use the same aroma, play the same background music, use the same words to let the baby know it's their bath time, bring awareness to your hands as you gently touch and hold your baby.

Of course, just like life, being predictable and consistent doesn't mean being rigid. Life changes, just as your baby's needs change (and yours), so create your little routine but allow for some flexibility too.

Rituals

Rituals transform routines into deeper connections. Rituals can provide you and your baby with an emotional sanctuary. When we mindfully create rituals we switch the routine from autopilot to meaningful mode, and that's where the true magic can happen.

Creating meaningful rituals is easy..... the key ingredient is consistency.

Here are a few ingredients you might like to choose as your ritual anchor:

- Songs and music
- Mantras
- Flowers and scents
- Water blessings

Songs and music

Singing has many developmental benefits for your baby's brain. Songs are a special type of speech and prepare a child's ear, voice, and brain for language. In the book *The Well Balanced Child*, Sally Goddard Blythe says "singing is particularly powerful in entertaining the listening and voicing skills which underlie spoken and written language."

Perhaps create *'your'* bathtime song, a little warm up that helps the baby know what's happening and that it's bathtime. Or why not play the same relaxing music in the background, it can become your bathtime song.

It's truly powerful if you have a particular relaxing song you used to play when you were pregnant. There has been much research to show that babies recognise the same music that was played a lot when they were developing in the womb. They pick up on the vibrations, the beat and tone. Studies have shown that music may have a part to play in brain development before birth - one famous study is by psychologist Frances Rauscher, called the Mozart Effect.

Simple bath time songs

"Are you happy, and are you ready? It's bathtime! Are you happy, and are you ready? It's bathtime!? Are you happy and ready, let's get changed, we are happy and ready now for bathtime!" (Perfect for bathtime beginnings)

Twinkle Twinkle little star *(perfect for floating)*

Twinkle Twinkle little star
Ears in the water
Tummy up high
Like a little star fish floating by

Row, Row, Your Boat *(perfect for sitting and swishing)*

Row row your boat
Gently down the stream
Merrily, merrily life is but a dream

A little space for your own bath time songs

Mantras and affirmations

The thoughts we say are our inner voice.
Thoughts become words and words become actions.
Words are so powerful, especially in and near water.

Chanting little mantras (words or sounds to carry vibrations around the body), can be extra special at bathtimes. The Japanese scientist, Emoto, discovered that the cellular structure of water can be changed by our words. This is such a powerful notion. When you are saying your little affirmations, know that the water will hold them, like little memories, imprinted in their cells.

Affirmations are little check in prompts:

- What am I grateful for?
- What one word can express how I feel?
- What do I need to let go of today?
- What feels challenging today?
- How can I hold myself with compassion?

The bath can become a safe and sacred space for you and your baby to practise acceptance, self-love, compassion, and to rest and unfold together.

Your 'words' will help you feel in sensory harmony with your baby during bathtime.

Words and thoughts for bathtime

> *"Bathtimes don't have to be perfect, because what matters is that we are together within this moment."*
> *"Today's bath will be simple, because simple is so much more."*
> *"I love you, I see you, I hear you, I believe in you, you are safe."*
> *"I am .....*

- Powerful
- The best mother/father/parent/carer
- A blessing to my baby
- Learning all the time
- Good enough

"With our splashy moments
We create happy moments,
With our happy moments
We share love"

A little space for you to share your own

Flowers and scents

Did you know our sense of smell is the only sense that is received by the brain directly, with no sensory filter? Our sense of smell is a powerful gateway to anchoring our emotions, as it's our limbic (the emotional part of our brains) that processes smells.

When using any baby product with scents, or room aromas, it is always my advice to use delicate and calming baby-friendly fragrances, like calamine or lavender.

In indigenous Japanese and Indian cultures, I have seen beautiful flower ceremonies offering and blessing the water with flowers. The water holds a delicate scent. However, I would like to offer a little note of caution when using scents etc. as a newborn baby's skin is very sensitive, so only the water is advised for bathing in the first few weeks.

If you would like to create your own little flower ceremonies, why not place a few flowers on your window sill, next to your candle. If it is just *your* bathtime, you can use a little gauze to hold your flowers, so they don't disperse.

> *Less is more for your baby, floating flowers in your baby's bath is not a good idea, and of course, everything is explored in your baby's mouth.*

Do you have a flower that is significant to your family?

In Hindu, puja is their worship ritual which means 'flower act'. Jasmine is often used as it signifies divine hope. Roses often signify love, and lilies peace.

As you place the flowers, set your intention. It could be one word, a phrase, or a little affirmation.

Water blessings

Blessing the water with your words will hold your emotions and intentions. Gratitude is one of the highest energy frequencies we can receive.

Giving thanks to the water, our family, life itself, or anything that is significant to you in this moment, will be held in the water.

> *"Thank you, water, our source of life. I love you, I love me."*

Blessing the water can be linked to your religious and spiritual beliefs, but it doesn't have to be. When we pause, we get to know ourselves.

> *Bless the water*
> *Bless ourselves*
> *Bless you Baby*
> *Bless everyone I hold dear in my heart*

The water has great powers to cleanse and heal.

I love to write little poems and blessings…….

> *"I honour myself, my life, and my dreams.*
> *I allow the water to wash away my worries.*
> *Feel the light in my heart, feel in flow."*
>
> *"The water helps me connect from within*
> *To simply be - ME*
> *No modern distractions to keep us apart*
> *A special moment in my heart."*

A little space for you

Let go of any worries
Allow the water to wash them away.
Be like water
Adaptable
Powerful
Full of flow.

CHAPTER 14

AND FINALLY ....

Whilst bathtime won't be the cure for all of life's wrinkles, it can make a difference to you and your baby.

Parenting can be challenging. Bathtimes can give you both a special time to relax and rest, which is much needed as a new parent. It can be a place to restore the balance physically, emotionally, and spiritually. To feel in sensory harmony.

Much advice for parents and caregivers often focuses on problems, with little help or solutions. Babies are often labelled as tricky, a cry baby, a windy baby etc. Bathing with your baby might bring you and your baby relief, and can often relieve digestive symptoms, with the added benefit that water times can promote sleep.

Don't be afraid to reach out to your family and friends if the delicate balance of life does become too hard. Don't struggle on alone.

Like the ocean, some baths will feel soft and slow, others will crash, splash, and feel loud. Both will be beautiful.

Meet Bubbles

Bath Babies is a special class, run by professional baby swim or baby massage teachers. Created by myself, Jo Wilson (the founder of Aqua Sensory), approved by the International Institute of Complementary Therapists (IICT) and recognised by many swim organisations across the world.

I saw there was a need to support parents and caregivers, to create a smoother transition from water times at home to the pool. Bath Babies classes are unique in every way. Classes are in little circles with babies enjoying their own bathtub. The focus is on exploring the water, combining nurturing touch rituals and practices with time to support you and your baby's wellbeing.

In our world today, we all need more love.

All your baby needs is your love.

The original "Love Bubble" ® was created by Gayle Berry at Blossom and Berry Massage. It is perfect as a reminder and to bring into your bath times.

The love bubble is an unconditional place, a sacred space where you can allow your love to emerge and deepen. There is much power in providing your baby with the time and space for them to unfold and grow in their own time, and own way.

Bathtimes can be your special, splashy place.

Enjoy and keep in touch, I would love to be here for you.

https://aquasensory.com/

Acknowledgements

Thank you from my heart, Christian Wilson, for your never-ending guidance. Birthing this book, you gave me the support I needed to keep going, along with the late night hot chocolate and solo parenting at times.

I reflected often on my knowledge and shared experiences. I would like to acknowledge the support from my aquatic connections, mentors, pioneers and cheerleaders. Thank you Kayle Burgham, Head of Aquatics at the Swimming Teachers Association, Ulrika Faerch from Happy Babies Swim, and Francoise Barbira Freedman, founder of Birthlight. And finally, but especially, Emmaline Kitson from Aqualight Babies, without you I would have not qualified to be a Baby Swim Teacher, which is my WHY and passion in life.

To my editor, Jo Macdonald, thank you for your expertise.

Mi Kelly from Admire Studios for the fantastic cover photography, and Baby Lara, our cover star.

My swim families from my swim school gave me so much inspiration for this book, along with my Bath Babies practitioners. To all the Baby Massage and Baby Swim Teachers out there, your kind words when I announced I was writing this book, spurred me on. I can't wait for you to share this book with your parents. Together we will make a difference.

About the Author

Jo Wilson is the founder of the child-development program *Aqua Sensory*, a Developmental Play Practitioner, and Aquatic Tutor. Jo has spoken at many International Aquatic Conferences, shaping early years swim programs across the world.

Jo lives in the UK with her husband, Christian, and two children, Kane and Millie, all water lovers. Jo runs two family swim centres with Christian in Warwickshire, all set up to provide an Aqua Sensory experience and ethos for learning to swim.

This is Jo's first book, which Jo promises to be one of many.

Bibliography and References

Chapter Three:
https://parentinfantfoundation.org.uk/1001-day
Winnicott, D, 1960. The Theory of the Parent-Infant Relationship. *International Journal of Psycho-Analysis.*

Chapter Five:
Hanscom A, 2016. *Balanced and Barefoot: How Unrestricted Outdoor Play Makes for Strong, Confident, and Capable Children,* New Harbinger

Chapter Six:
Poem written in collaboration with Sophia Michalopoulou at Water Happy.
http://www.waterhappy.net/

Wallace J Nichols, 2015. *Blue Mind: The Surprising Science That Shows How Being Near, In, On, or Under Water Can Make You Happier, Healthier, More Connected, and Better at What You Do.* Back Bay Books

Chapter Nine:
https://www.sciencenews.org/blog/growth-curve/staring-baby-eyes-brain-waves-sync

Chapter Ten:
Cerebral motor function in very premature-at-birth adolescents: a brain stimulation exploration of kangaroo mother care effects. C. Schneider (2012)

Chapter Thirteen:
https://www.thewatermain.org/blog/the-water-ritual
Goddard Blyth, S. (2005) *The Well Balanced Child: Movement and Early Learning.* Hawthorn Press

https://www.aptaclub.co.uk/pregnancy/bonding-and-development/pregnancy-music-the-effect-on-unborn-babies.html

Emoto, M. (2004) *The Hidden Messages in Water,* Beyond Words Publishing.

Chapter Fourteen:
https://www.blossomandberry.com/

Baby and Swim Books I love:
Gerhardt, S. (2004) *Why love Matters,* Routledge

Faerch U. (2018) Happy Babies Swim: Creating Stronger Relationships Between Parents and Children Through the Gift of Swim

Freedman, F. (2001) *Water Babies: Teach Your Baby the Joys of Water,* Lorenz Books